POWELLOGY

Jonathan Powell

POWELLOGY

©2016 Jonathan Powell

ISBN: 978-1-940244-82-2

All rights reserved. No part of this book may be reproduced in any form or by any electronic or mechanical means, including information storage and retrieval systems, without permission in writing from the author, except by a reviewer, who may quote brief passages in review.

cover design by
207Branding.com

photography by
Photographer Patrick Jones

interior book design and production by
Indie Author Warehouse
Thomaston, Maine
www.indieauthorwarehouse.com

Printed in the United States of America

To my sainted great-grandmother, who gave me a ground to stand upon; my strong father and sweet mother for giving me their name when I was without one; and to my children, who give me the hope of an incredible future filled with love and acceptance. Thank you for letting me be your dad.

Acknowledgments

To KATRINA JEFFERSON: You told me, "Do it," and you created from that, and I will never forget it.

APRIL COHEN: You believed in this vision and wouldn't allow me to let it go until it manifested, and for that I will never forget. (Thanks, EARL, for being a Pastor.)

DR. E. BERNARD JORDAN: Thank you for unlocking the gift of light for me.

To my gifted and gracious leaders ARCHBISHOP ROY E. BROWN and DEBORAH CROWE: Thank you for letting me be **me** and still loving me.

To DR. CARLTON PEARSON: Your life and courage (along with your fried collard greens) have been a gift to us all.

DARIUS NIXON: Thank you for sharing your mind and approach to this thing we call life.

DR IONA E LOCKE thank you for your tender motherly encouragement and fireside chats.

DRS CECIL and ROSE ANN PRATT you both covered me and protected me from all of the lions and bears and I'll never forget that.

"We don't get harmony when *everybody* sings the same note. Only notes that are *different* can harmonize. The same is true with *people*."

—Steven Goodier

POWELLOGY

CHAPTER ONE:
FLOETRY

"The door from the next room suddenly opened with a timid, quiet creak, as if thus announcing the entrance of a very insignificant person…"
—Fyodor Dostoyevsky, *The Double*

I've always loved this particular passage from *The Double* by Dostoyevsky. *The Double* tells the story of a government clerk who goes mad. It explores the internal psychological struggle of its main character, Yakov Petrovich Golyadkin, who keeps meeting someone who is his exact double in appearance, but who inwardly possesses all the personality strengths he wishes he had. He meets a fully expressed version of himself in someone else. The version we often daydream about being—the one who would walk into the lunchroom cafeteria and capture everyone's attention—that moment when time and space disappears and all eyes are on us, and people gaze at not just how attractive we are physically, but also at our effortless wealth of personality.

My mind paints a picture of "the door" that suddenly opens for the entrance of Insignificance.

How many of us enter the door onto the stage of life wondering if we will be considered insignificant?

There is a famous line from Shakespeare's *As you Like It*, Act II Scene VII: "All the world's a stage, and all the men and women merely players; they have their exits and their entrances, and one man in his time plays many parts."

We all have entrances and exits, but it is essential that we have an assurance that our entrances and exits mean something so significant that we are never forgotten. Perhaps one of our greatest fears is going through this entire experience and totally missing the true essence of why we are here.

The water that fills a river has a steady and continuous flow. The geographical location of the river does not matter. The flow is all; the flow is what makes the water significant to the river. Such is the truth of life. Life has a flow. Every human being has a different flow. And the fact that no two people have the same flow reminds us of the astounding beauty of individualism.

Years ago, my mother took my brother, my sister, and me up to visit my grandmother in a small town in upstate New York called Glens Falls—South Glens Falls to be exact—which is not very far from Lake George. If you've never been there, it's a beautiful place to behold in the summertime. While we were there, we visited one of the lakes, and she did something that, at that moment, seemed utterly miraculous. At that time,

I was only ten, but nothing about that lake experience escaped me; I still remember it vividly. My mother took a stone and tossed it into the water. Unexpectedly, the stone started to skip across the surface as if it had mutated into a creature with legs. I remember trying to imagine how many legs the stone must have to be able to move so fast across this water without sinking.

But after the skipping came something that amazed me even further. I noticed that the stone left ripples in the lake, and the ripples produced a unique rhythm, a flow that extended beyond where the stone initially touched the water. Witnessing this sight instigated a peculiar thought: life is the water, the stones are us and those we encounter, and the ripples are the distinctive aftermath of our experiences.

WHAT IS YOUR RHYTHM?

There are a couple of different aspects to the concept of the ripple, but the one that is most relevant to me right now is its rhythm. All of life has rhythm; it has a peculiar flow and a consistent movement. For many of us, however, the challenge is realizing what the rhythm is and coming into synchronization with it. I think there might even be a well-known song about the rhythm of life out there somewhere in musicland. Anyway, life has a rhythm, and when we're not in accordance with that rhythm, the consequence is being offbeat in everything we do. Your life's rhythm sets the tone for everything in your personal world.

Routines are established through our rhythms. Just ponder your daily process of doing things, and I'm sure you'll agree that the majority of your functioning is wrapped up in your routines. Take, for example, preparation for your workday. You have a set time to wake up, an allotted time to shower, dress, and get out of the house to arrive at your workplace by a certain time. Everything is precisely mapped out, including your commute to work. What happens when something doesn't go according to the plan and the flow is disturbed? It throws everything off, and, more than likely, you will find yourself upset and frustrated. Not necessarily because you can no longer go to work, or even because you'll be reprimanded for showing up a little late—but simply because the flow has been interrupted, and you're now offbeat. Once you become accustomed to dancing to the beat of a certain drum, readjusting, especially against your own preference, can be overwhelming.

There are routines and there are relationships.... both are byproducts of life's flow.

The chance to establish relationships is one of the primary elements in this journey as human beings. The relationships in whichc we become invested can color our environment with great joy or unbearable pain; they can flood the shore of our surroundings with bliss or leave us despondent and resentful. In either instance, a large part of life is relationships, and they too have a specific rhythm. To decide to connect with someone is also to decide to learn and become part of their rhythm, and at some point, to create a rhythm that is exclusive to that relationship.

Relationships and rhythm remind me of double-dutch. Sounds bizarre, doesn't it? Well, let me elaborate for clarity's sake. Back when I was younger, and I'm sure you can relate, kids used to play double-dutch. In this game, there are two people turning two ropes in order to create a certain motion and rhythm while the jumper is on the outside observing what the rhythm is. Once she grasps it, she jumps in and follows the pattern.

Do you see the connection now as it pertains to relationships? Before jumping in, you have to allocate time to learning and observing the other person's patterns and rhythm. What speed are they moving at? Is it a speed that you can keep up with? What's their personality? Is their character compatible with yours? These questions will help you do what the jumper does in a game of double-dutch—study the rhythm and then jump. You never just leap into the ropes simply because they're turning; you study first.

An impulsive decision is dangerous and almost always promises regret. The reason, I think, that no one just jumps into a rope without thinking when playing double-dutch is primarily because they understand the risks that come with it. This same caution should be applied with our relationship-building. The rule of thumb is simple: know what the rhythm is before you jump into the flow.

Moment of Introspection: *Based on all that you've read so far, can you identify what your personal rhythm is? What works for you? What are your daily systems for work, relationships, and the like?*

FEAR FIGHTS THE FLOW

Earlier today, I was at the pool with my kids in the park. There I saw a little boy who had to be eight or nine years old. As he was playing, fully engulfed in his pool activity, I noticed his eyes; they were full of adventure and utterly fearless. I was astonished to see how his eyes soaked up the reality of every moment. It seemed that, with every second that went by, his eyes enlarged as if to match the moment he was presently in.

It was delightful to see a child living without a filter to block or interfere with the reality of what was; it left no room for fear to gain access. Once fear shows up on the scene, everything is at its mercy…and that is not at all a good thing. Fear makes everything more than it should be. Minors become majors; falsehoods seem factual. Why? Because fear is the ultimate creator of illusions. It will cause you to over-think things and convince you that taking any risks will guarantee failure, all the while jeopardizing the flow meant for you.

Fear is one of the biggest lies that we believe.

As long as fear exists, your flow will be stifled, or even more detrimental, it will become blocked. When you're fighting against fear, you have to be strategic. The way to win against fear is by not believing the lies that it offers. Instead, you have to see things for what they are while being optimistic; you have to make a sound decision to enjoy the flow of your moment. Period. The little boy in the park was optimistic, adventurous, and full of hope about where he was and what he was doing. So even if fear that he might possibly drown or suffer an injury in the pool was a thought in his mind, you couldn't tell because he was too busy being engulfed in the fun—enjoying the flow of the present—to entertain anything else.

That's the deal with fear: you can't entertain it even if it's present. Never should our goal be to avoid fear—that's not possible anyway—but we should resist it so that it doesn't win control.

The soap opera, *One Life to Live*, is a true testament to its title. When a life is not lived, is it really life? Or is it mere existence? When we're not flowing and dancing with life, when we're not at one with that flow because of fear, are we really living or are we just dead men walking?

All great humanitarians, philosophers, musicians, and artists became one with life and said something like, "Even though I should be afraid and even though it hasn't been done before, I'll dance anyway." That's what it's about—being able to make a decision to dance anyway. Life is playing a special tune and waiting on you to simply go with the flow. You may not be the greatest dancer, and everything on the dance floor may not emulate perfection, but dance anyway.

What life is trying to pull out of us is a gift to humanity. The ripples that sparked your flow reach so far and wide that they touch a different time, a different space, a different existence that once was a mystery. But the ripples won't be ignited until you live life. Creation happens when life is lived and a flow emerges. When that flow takes place and you become one with the rhythm, you'll see things happen that you didn't anticipate. You'll see that things will come to you. You'll learn that fear was just an illusion. You'll realize that relationships are worth the risk, regardless of any fear you may have of being insignificant or forgotten.

I often say that what you want wants you, which is why you have a desire for it. Our attractions are innate, not coincidental. What you're requesting is requesting you, which is why you're requesting it. We have an appetite for things, and it's really the universe's way of letting us know we're supposed to have them. But because we're so afraid of getting into a rhythm that may defy our logic, we never pursue our desires.

Following the rhythm will contradict the filters that you've placed over your listening and your seeing eyes and ears because they don't fit logically into the frame of the world that we live in. But there is no frame in which life has to be lived. There are no rules that life has to be given. There were rules that told Martin Luther King Jr. and Mahatma Gandhi that they could not achieve their dreams. Yet, both broke those rules, went against the grain, and created unprecedented greatness—all because they became one with the rhythm and the flow of their life. Your life has a rhythm and flow, but until you become one with that flow, there will be no creation. Nothing new will manifest until you trust your heart enough to do something different, something that's outside your normal routine.

There will be no synergy in the life you live because you're fighting what is naturally you. You're fighting what the universe has gifted you with and made you capable of achieving because you're afraid of the flow, afraid to see what's on the other side of taking a risk. But why? Is it because you fear failure? If so, change your thinking. Failure is only a state of mind. You only fail when you don't find the lesson in what didn't go right or what didn't go your way. When you walk away with a lesson, that lesson becomes your power.

As I mentioned before, fear is one of the greatest blocks to the flow of life. When I think of things flowing, especially water, I think of a dam. Dams are used to control the flow. But when it comes to life, control and flow constitute an oxymoron; because how can a flow be controlled? Isn't it supposed to move freely?

Often we try to regulate our flow so we're accepted in the society or culture in which we live. For example, if I grew up in a conservative environment, even though I might have liberal ideas, I will try to constrain those liberal ideas within the framework of my background. Yet, that very thing goes against the flow that is natural for me. We have a bad habit of conforming instead of creating. We're conformists when we were born to be artists. That must change. That change begins with dismissing fear, and culminates in following our distinct flow.

YOUR FLOW IS FREEDOM FOR SOMEONE ELSE

Flow is about being fully self-expressed to such a degree that, even if your environment does not support your flow, you emerge from it and create a new environment that demonstrates "this is how I move and this is the world I have created."

Almost nothing is as liberating as self-expression. When you're able to fully stand in the truth of who you are with bold confidence, you're functioning at the highest level of self. As you continue to evolve into who you truly are, that liberation becomes tangible and transferable to those in your sphere of influence. Your freedom will bring self-expression to others.

If we are where we are supposed to be in the universe, we free others from the boundaries that restrict them. We remove the dams from the places that reduce people to controlled flows instead of creative flows.

When you deal with your dam, you also have to deal with who is controlling the dam. If the dam is being controlled by someone else, that means they're in control of your life, and in control of your self-expression. How dangerous is your existence when a mortal being controls your mortality? What kind of genocide can emerge when other powers, subject to the same laws of gravity and humanity as you, control others to the point that they govern how much life will be lived, how much expression will be expressed, or how much existence will exist? When we understand this concept, we begin to understand the reason for breaking dams. Dams only damn us to an existence that is limited and unfulfilling.

We've been restricted to limited positions and lifestyles long enough. Fear is holding us back and impeding our ability to evolve to the fullest of our divine flow. The buck stops here! The responsibility to place an expiration date on fear is yours and no one else's. You have to be the one to rescue your flow from the deadly grip of fear. If you don't, the dam will continue to rule your flow. If you don't, you won't create anything new. If you don't, you'll always do what culture and society say, and never what your heart desires.

But if you do,
everything changes,
everything starts to flow,
everything begins to adjust to your harmony.
If you do, the waters will flow so profusely, so strongly.

CONCLUSION

You've probably already realized by now that the message of this chapter, and that of the overall book, is very simple: to get you to break down the dams in your life so you can have a free flow. Sometimes in examining the flow—or flowology, if you like—you'll notice that in order to get to the destination the flow is carrying you to, you will have to learn and master the art of submission. It's not the easiest thing to do, and it will probably require the dismantling of your pride; however, it's worth whatever it takes. After all, how far has fighting the flow or listening to your fears carried you?

Going with the flow means resisting the urge to have to understand everything before you submit to what's going on. Many times, it's better to move with the universe and trust that it won't lead you astray. As you move with the evolution and flow, you'll find yourself being transported to places and experiences that you would never have otherwise encountered had you first demanded to fully understand all the details.

A lot of times, we have minds full of ideas that depict how things should be, who people should be, where we should be, and how successful we should be by a certain point. We come up with the plan and say, "Well, I'll do four years of college here; I'll do my graduate work here, and then I will get married. I'll be married for two years, then have some kids, and we'll move from here to this next place. Then, we'll buy a summer home in this area." Our mind is the creator of fantasies and expectations that we spend our whole lives trying to accomplish. But most times, none of those things match our life's fabric, and as a consequence, we end up dancing to the beat of the wrong drum instead of submitting to our own flow. "What screws us up the most in Life is the picture in our head of how it's supposed to be"

On the contrary, some of us are patterning our journeys based on what we see happening to those around us. Covetousness! Coveting is the bad habit of wanting something only because you witness someone else with it. Benjamin Franklin said it this way: "It is the eye of other people that ruins us. If I were blind I would want neither fine clothes, fine houses, or fine furniture." In other words, we only want what we want because we see others with it. Want only creates more want. Once you have something that you've wanted, you then move on to wanting something else. This is perhaps why the scriptures indicate, "The Lord is my shepherd, I shall not want." This issue isn't really with wanting, it's with wanting what others have, not because it's meaningful for us, but because we covet it. Consequently, we find that when we get those things, they're not satisfying.

Now, I'm in no way suggesting that we shouldn't have plans or desires for our life. In fact, I'm of the persuasion that without a plan, you're essentially setting yourself up for a series of failures. But in addition to a plan, you have to leave room for things that aren't included in the plan to fit in. It's usually those things that change our life in amazing ways.

Do you see why it's so much more rewarding to just figure out your flow and go with that?

All of this makes me think of a moment in Alexandre Dumas's novel, *The Count of Monte Cristo*, which tells the story of a man who is wrongly accused of a crime he did not commit. When the protagonist Edmond Dantes eventually finds himself free and enormously wealthy, he takes it upon himself to act the role of Providence, rewarding those who helped him in his plight and punishing those responsible for his years of agony. This, in my opinion, is what breeds most of the issues that many of us are dealing with. Because we've fought the flow and gone for what we thought was meant for us—or what we wanted to be for us—it had left us with more problems than pleasure, or even turned us into monsters of a sort. When you fight the flow, when you fight floetry, when you don't work with the poetry of the universe, a deep ambivalence will begin to grow because of dissatisfaction.

Many of you reading this are dissatisfied because what you assumed would reward you with peace hasn't succeeded at doing so. In *The Count of Monte Cristo*, Edmond Dantes finds that after he exacts the revenge he was hoping for, he's still in the same place—very dissatisfied—because satisfaction is not found in things or money or revenge. Satisfaction is found in the flow. In my own experiences, I have found that even in the deepest and darkest of caves, when I have been confused and completely bewildered, there is somehow a growing peace that sits there and keeps me company. As long as you work with the flow, rather than fighting it, you'll discover that you'll get to a place that you did not know existed. You'll get somewhere that only the flow could have carried you.

When you examine the sand on a beach, every grain of sand there has been transported from another place. Why? Because the sand did not fight the flow. The sand reached the shore but it didn't originate there. If the grains of sand could tell us a story, I imagine they would tell us that where they began and where they ended are two different places; they'd tell us of the many waters they encountered before hitting the shore. Sand travels hundreds and thousands of miles to get to the shore where it settled. Similarly, there are waters designed to usher us to an expected destination.

    I'm convinced that if you move with the flow of the universe, just like the sand, you'll find your distinctive shore. This shore will be flooded with personified dreams and realities far wilder and greater than anything you could have gotten by not going with the flow. That is exactly what floetry is all about.

"Action springs not from THOUGHT, but from a READINESS for responsibility"
—Dietrich Bonhoeffer

CHAPTER TWO:
BECAUSE

The entire purpose is the "why."
The passions are the "how."
The product is the "what."

GOD! GOD! GOD! The chances are that when I—or anyone else—proclaim this name, it immediately opens a Pandora's box. Greek mythology has always intrigued me, especially the story of "Pandora's Box." In Greek mythology, Pandora is the first woman on earth. She is endowed with gifts from all of the elite and superior gods and goddesses. Apollo blessed her with music; Aphrodite "shed grace upon her head." Zeus gives to Pandora a jar, or pithos (jar). He commands her emphatically: DO NOT OPEN THE JAR! But as often is the case, her curiosity causes her to crack open the lid. And from the box spews every damnable evil and trouble known to humanity. Pain, sickness, strife and an innumerable amount of adverse ills become a part of the human experience. Pandora manages to close the lid and trap one spirit in the jar (or box). A shy almost skittish spirit named Elpis which is usually translated as "hope." That is what makes and causes a stirring of emotions when the name God is mentioned. His name offers the idea of Hope to so many, and yet leaves us full of questions, ideas, fears, pains, judgments, theories, and a litany of other things. There is no other name on earth that can demand such endless reactions and rouse such countless emotions each time it is mentioned. Yes, there are many great names that belong to some very powerful beings, and when their name is called, that can cause an array of reactions and emotions that range from horror to excitement. Yet no name can do what the name(s) of God does. And perhaps that is the greatest reason to say it, believe it, and trust it.

More than anything else, my hope is not to convince anyone to own my personal conviction as it pertains to God. However, my aim is to introduce a perspective for consideration, a perspective that can effectively compel one to discover the unique necessity of God.

Rob Bell shares something profound in his book, *What We Talk About When We Talk About God*: "Like a mirror, God appears to be more and more a reflection of whoever it is that happens to be talking about God at the moment." That realization is pretty awesome and rather alarming at the same time, wouldn't you agree? Just think about it. The image of God, an immortal, supernatural power, can be determined by a person (a mortal being) who is speaking of God in a particular moment. On one hand, this can be amazing, because if the person speaking is representing God in an appropriate manner, it's a great image. If not? Well, that's not good at all.

That in itself opens the door to the many versions of God. Even though there is only one God, the different representations of him present various versions that people attempt to understand and know of their own accord. It is that particular idea that leads us to this interesting story in Jewish tradition concerning the Genesis.

It is a fascinating story...

Here you have God, who begins with the creation of the Universe; and then, by some interesting means, in Genesis 1:26 (MSG) God speaks: "Let us make human beings in our image, make them reflecting our nature so they can be responsible for the fish in the sea, the birds in the air, the cattle, And, yes, Earth itself, and every animal that moves on the face of Earth." God created human beings; he created them godlike, reflecting the very essence and nature of God.

And there we have it...or so we think. As I fast forwarded to the next chapter of the same book, I saw something that I had never really paid attention to. (How often does that happen?) In Genesis 2:7 (MSG), God forms man out of dirt from the ground and blows the breath of life into his nostrils. In that instant, man comes alive—a living, breathing, moving soul!

So, check this out:

Chapter 1—God Creates

Chapter 2—God Forms

From the onset, I was always under the impression that Chapter 1 was all there was on the subject of creation and how human existence came into play, but clearly that's not the case. The story didn't stop at God *creating the idea of human beings;* it went all the way to *formation.*

Considering this, it is very possible to *create* ideas, visions, dreams, and even opportunities but never see them actually *form* into anything more concrete than thoughts. In creation form, an idea is a mere mental picture, something that fills up the spaces of your imagination. When it is actually formed, it becomes a physical manifestation of what was once a thought. You and I were once mental pictures in the mind of God. The moment he took dirt and conceived us and provided us with the breath of life, we became tangible beings.

What is often so frustrating for us is having an idea…and not being able to make it reality. The truth is, dreaming isn't the problem for a lot of people. It's easy to dream, it's easy to have an idea that is game-changing and innovative. But trying to produce something of those dreams? Now, that's the struggle! That's the part of the process that tears people down and discourages them in their pursuit to form their thoughts.

While cruising my Instagram feed, I found these words: "What screws us up most in life is the picture in our head of how it is supposed to be." Is this true for you?

There is no doubt that most of the confusion we encounter happens in the space of transitioning. That's the space in which we attempt to take a thought we have created and form it into something tangible. When your mind has processed something a particular way for an extensive period of time, attempting to break away from that perspective is strenuous. It's even more daunting to have to break away from that perspective because you have absolutely no means of making anything of it.

Many of you have in your mind what kind of mate you desire, the amount of money you need, the job you wish to have, the places you want to travel, the legacy you wish to leave behind, and so on. Yet, you feel stuck with a person…stuck with a job…stuck making a certain amount of money…and stuck in a place that doesn't match the level of passion you feel inside. Have you ever felt prisoner to a *choice* or *decision* so much so that you're unsure of how to move to the next phase?

IT'S TIME TO TURN WHAT'S IN YOUR HEAD INTO WHAT YOU CAN TOUCH

In the same book where God is doing all of this magnificent creating and forming, making creation, and finding harmony in reality, he gives the newly formed man a strict directive that's found in Genesis 2:16-17 (MSG). God commands, "You can eat from any tree in the garden except the Tree of Knowledge of Good and Evil. Don't eat from it. The moment you eat from that tree, you're dead."

In other words, don't eat it or you're GOING TO GET IT! But why? That's the question I immediately asked as a young child sitting in Sunday school, and even now, as I have probed into this ancient story, the question lingers on. Why? Why? Why? Yet, the only answer I can conjure up or somehow contextualize is: "Because I said so." The Bible was written many, many centuries ago. However, if it had been written in 21st century vernacular, I'm confident that God would have put it just like that, "Because I said so." Exclaimed with sovereignty and authority, that's the answer God would render to my inquiry.

Bear with me as I have a flashback moment here. As a ten-year-year old kid growing up in my hometown of Bay Shore, Long Island, nothing was more exciting to me than going out with my friends to play down the street after a long day of school and doing whatever homework I was given. However, there was always an impeding barrier to my "fun time" due to my saintly mother. When I would ask to go out with my friends to play, she would always deflect the question with "Go ask your father." It never failed. Out of all of the things she could say in response to my request, those words were the most chilling and shuddery. Why? I was terrified of my father. It wasn't because he was a horrible father figure, but because he was a massive force of punishment and authority. As a kid, my dad was a giant with the strength of a Roman legion and a booming voice that shook trees and made the souls of lions shudder. I would do whatever it took to be as far away from him as possible, so talking or asking questions was out of the question, due to the fact I hated to hear "No."

It would literally take me an entire 45 minutes to conjure up enough courage to creep down the hall like a mouse walking by an alley full of cats, just to ask if I could go outside or do something fun. In fact, I had to follow this same process regardless of what I wanted to ask him. I hated having to jump through so many hoops to get what I wanted, but I did. Absolutely reluctantly and fear-filled, but I did it. Time and time again, my fearful self would ask, "Daddy, can I go down the street to play?" only to hear him say "No." For some reason, I'd always ask, "Why?" and he would answer, as only a parent could: "Because I said so!" And of course, that was the end of that discussion.

"Because I said so!" Those words, I promise you, became absolutely present to me at a young age, probably due to the fact that there was never a need or an opportunity for further discussion after that "Because" moment. That remark was definitive and final. There was no way to get around it; I had to take it for what it was worth and make myself become okay with it. Once it was spoken, it settled the idea, the question, and the response. Period!

I must admit that when I became a father, one of the things I secretly enjoyed was doling out that wonderful phrase to my kids. It seemed so powerful; it's like a sweet confirmation or reminder that I'm grown, in control, and have total authority over what I allow and disallow for my children. At that time, it was simply about power, which is always a great motivator for many young teenagers. But now, it's deeper than that. Since I've acquired some grey in my hair, things have become a little different. I notice that the same word is still powerful, but in a more relevant and rewarding way now. Prior to maturation, I thought "Because" was a badge of honor for the grown-up; I thought it was a statement of dictatorship that removed the need to have to explain oneself. Yet, before I knew it, I somehow discovered that the word had much more meaning and involvement than the shallow matters I once filtered it through.

My present filter for this phrase is: "Be Cause." It's that simple.

Instead of using "because" as an excuse for not doing something—to dictate, to justify, or to avoid offering an explanation—I perceive the words as an invitation to experience a better quality and significance for life. The word, for me, is actually an invitation "to be (the) cause...in the manner of life.... your own life." In this regard, it's not about anyone else; it's about you and your life, and what matters to your passions and purpose. Life could take on a brand new meaning and new possibility if you would only be (the) cause in every happening of your life.

What does it mean to be the cause? It means becoming the reality you want to see. It means forsaking every excuse to pursue what matters. It means stopping at nothing to see all that you dream and imagine. It is so easy to find reasons to resign from moving into action.

I'm overweight. I'm single.

I'm broke. I'm divorced.

I'm uneducated. I'm unattractive. I'm not like them.

But there's no fulfillment to be found in running away from being the cause of your life. If you should spend your whole life without making anything inside of you tangible, what would that say of your character? How would that reflect the God that shaped you in his image?

Now is the time for you to take on the mindset God used in Genesis. He saw a need for something he wanted that did not exist in the world around him. And what did he do? He created and formed it. He decided to be the cause. He used the passion he felt toward what was missing to tap into his creative power. What are you waiting for? That same creative power is at work in you; you inherited it even before conception.

Gone are the days of tired excuses. Think of it this way: every excuse you can imagine and create have all, at one time or another, been used by someone else. And many of those people have in some way or another, beat the odds and accomplished the goal that was set before them. However, that only happens when a person takes ownership of their life and says, "I will be the cause in all matters." You have to come to a place where you decided to *become* by *causing*. Become better by causing change. Become great by causing a compelling work ethic. Become what you're ambitious about by causing effective plans and decisions. To cause simply means to create and form.

I'm sure you've heard the famous mantra, "Life is 90% what happens and 10% how you react to it." It's the small 10% that makes the difference. It's you stepping outside of your comfort zone in order to truly become "grown." People won't give you anything and, in all actuality, they owe you nothing. You have the power to make things; you have the power to create and you have the power to form! Do you know why? In the words of the creator in Genesis: *"Be Cause!"*

"The limits of my LANGUAGE means the limit of my WORLD!"

—Ludwig Wittgenstein

CHAPTER THREE:
BI

Lao Tzu said, "When I let go of what I am,
I become what I might be." What true words!
What we may be...
What we could be...
What we should be...

The possibilities are endless, yet there is a risk involved, and one with cataclysmic proportions. We must be willing to let go of ourselves, and that is no easy task especially given our unhealthy commitment to the "*know-ness*" of our existence. Most of our lives are spent as pseudo-epistemologists, collecting and analyzing knowledge so we may respond and react without ever becoming one with the actual experience. We miss the opportunity for true growth and self-actualization by processing and spitting out data yet never truly relating to anything.

What I am and who I am are entirely different. It is completely possible to be locked into what you are with all good intentions, and yet miss your entire purpose for being on this earth. Pressure is normally the cause for people selling out to "what I might be." The pressure of...

> Family
> Society
> Expectations

They all contribute to the great sellout that results in our reducing ourselves to fit into molds not meant to house our brand of impeccability. Being boxed in and living a diluted existence is one of the most devastating things that can happen to a human being.

Over time, I became extremely aware of the fact that one of the most prevalent challenges in our relationships with one another is our inability to communicate effectively; and one of the reasons this challenge exists is because we all speak different languages, and most of us do not understand a language that differs from our own or we do not care to learn another language.

Men and women speak different languages.

Ethnic groups speak different languages.

Children and adults speak different languages.

African Americans speak English differently than Caucasians.

Americans speak English differently than British.

Americans speak English and French speak French.

The point I'm conveying here?

The world is colored by different languages. It's our responsibility to learn them.

THE NOD

I was watching a new ABC series a couple of weeks ago called *Blackish*. One of the characters is an African-American boy who lives a high-class suburban life. One day, at school with his father, he crossed paths with one of his friends. Neither one of them acknowledged the other. Startled by their obvious disregard for each other's presence, the father couldn't understand it. In his day, the common way to greet someone was with a nod of the head; it was a universal code that black people use to acknowledge each other's existence. Because this didn't happen, the father realized that the young men did not know how to communicate with each other, According to the father, all Black people knew the universal code of the "NOD" as the sign of acknowledging each other's existence. The failure to acknowledge was epically baffling to the young man's father. He found it totally baffling.

One of the interesting things about "the nod" is how much emphasis we put on certain kinds of communication and how the lack of communication can affect us. Yet, how many of us move into action to correct this lack?

For many people, it's not that we don't love each other. A lack of communication isn't always a lack of love. (I might add, though, that communication is absolutely a function of love.)

More often than not, it's simply proof that, somewhere along the way, we did not put enough effort into exploring the language, personality, and mind of the one(s) we are in relationship with. That's a real epidemic these days. Everyone is connected but few are truly invested in who the other is beneath the surface. Our social media platforms give us a false sense of intimacy. We swipe left or right for a match on Tinder, we post pictures to see how many likes we can get on Instagram, and we do our best to bare our souls with 140 characters on Twitter. But do we truly know? Do we really "get" the people we are in relationships with? Do we venture into their hidden or dark places? Or do we just settle for what looks good or sounds good to our ever-evolving culture?

CHANEL vs. SKITTLES

I can remember years ago when I was in a particular relationship, one that was really promising and exciting. My girlfriend and I had a great connection with one another. We had grown with each other and had many similarities. It was Valentine's Day, our first Valentine's Day together, so I approached it with the intention of making it memorable. Everything had to be perfect; everything had to be better than anything my significant other had ever experienced.

So I pulled out all of the stops. My creative juices were flowing, and I did everything I thought would make this one for the books. I found a five-star hotel and had chocolates spread nicely across the bed. There were beautiful roses and quality champagne. Later that evening, we went to dine at a restaurant which had a violinist playing warm, romantic melodies.

And then the night got interesting…

When she gave me my Valentine's Day gift, a bottle of cologne, I felt an immediate loss of power and a slight disappointment. It was not because I had a problem with the Chanel cologne. No, my issue was that I felt she didn't understand me, that despite all the time spent together, our connection was not as strong as I'd believed and hoped. Again, the cologne was great, and the gesture was certainly appreciated. And just so you don't think that I'm some high-maintenance guy who's impossible to please, let me go on record by saying that receiving the gift made me feel appreciated. However, if she had truly *known* me, she would have been aware of my love for Wild Berry Skittles or gifted me with CDs from my favorite teacher or speaker. It wasn't about quantity or expense, but rather the quality of thought involved in the gift. That in itself is a reflection of knowing and communicating with others.

Do you notice that the word "communication" has within its clutches the word "commune?" What does it mean to commune? Simply to be one with something or someone.

Nothing is quite as conflicting as feeling appreciated while also feeling misunderstood. So often we don't know what is important to our partner, and as a result, we try to predispose and predetermine and say to ourselves, "You know what you need and you know what you want, so I'm going to give you what I think you want and what I think you need." This is problematic for one major reason: when you rely solely on your thoughts to determine certain factors of your relationship, you almost always reach the wrong conclusion. To remedy this, it's wise to simply pursue the knowledge that allows you to successfully honor the needs, desires, and expectations of your relationship—in other words, to learn the other's language. This is the practice of masterful communication.

THE DANGER OF FAILING TO KNOW THEIR LANGUAGE

The lovely lady who gave me the Chanel cologne had a defining moment in front of her to prove that she knew my language, and she mismanaged it. The gesture was kind but disappointing. It is from these disappointments that unspoken ambivalences emerge. One of the greatest dangers of failing to know—or failing to prove you know—someone's language is animosity. If you know anything about animosity, especially the kind that manifests as silence rather than confrontation, you know it is the launching pad for damage and despair.

Every time you fail to tap into the language of someone with whom you're in relationship, you're running a huge risk. Let me help you with a simple, yet practical example: babies.

Babies have a unique language of their own; it's simple, but if you're not one to pay attention to detail, you risk not meeting their needs. For instance, most babies will whine when they are hungry, sleepy, or need changing. Although their whining can indicate a variety of needs, one thing's for sure: they're in need of attention and care. Adults, likewise, have their own "whine," and it will indicate that they're expecting, needing, and wanting something.

But what happens when you ignore the whine of a baby? That whine becomes a loud cry, and if some time passes by without him getting what he's yearning for, it may very well turn into kicking and screaming, what we call a temper tantrum. Though the analogy references children and babies, how many of you are aware of the temper tantrums you have witnessed or have yourself thrown? I'll let you think about it.

Your significant other also has a reaction to the experience of unmet expectations, needs, and wants. Their version of a "loud cry" or "kicking and screaming" could translate into many things, especially if it becomes a perpetual reality. For the first few episodes, they may be willing to tolerate feeling neglected and misunderstood. But after that, you may be entering into a danger zone that probably won't be favorable to the relationship.

LANGUAGE LEARNING HAS TO BE RECIPROCAL

There's one thing that must be crystal clear: it's not just about you. To think that everyone should learn your language—and you should learn no one else's—is absolutely selfish. It has to be an equal exchange; otherwise it won't be effective. One of my favorite artists, Lauryn Hill penned these words in her song, Ex-Factor: "Tell me who I have to be to get some reciprocity." Too often we are selfishly locked in our own way of thinking and communication. There's an old adage: The Golden Rule tells us to treat others the way that we wish to be treated. This simple principle adage would prevent the failure of a lot of relationships if it was put into consistent practice. You can't demand that a person sacrifice their time and vulnerability to learn who you are unless you plan to do the same for them.

No one learns how to speak in a certain way just to be able to understand and engage with others. Another goal is to be understood and connected with. We are meant to be creatures of reciprocity. Love and relationship are built on the premise of give and take, not take and take. When take and take is the approach, relationships become one-sided. Whatever is one-sided doesn't last long and will eventually come crashing down on you.

If you're a selfish communicator, you're probably used to hearing things like, "I feel like you're not listening to me" or "I feel like what you said/did was rude and selfish." These are common phrases spoken by someone who feels there is no recognition or regard, no reciprocity, for what they say or how they feel. Sometimes, it's a misunderstanding, but most often these feelings are hurtful realities that exist because there is indeed a selfish communicator in the equation.

Moment of Introspection: *Are you a selfish communicator? How intentional are you about making sure that you're learning, respecting, and meeting others on the level of their own language?*

When it comes to communication, aim to be more present, more sensitive, and more mindful. If you want to unlock the deepest places of someone's love, show them that their language matters to you. Show them that inviting you into their world wasn't a mistake or a wasted gesture. In return, they'll show you that accepting their invitation wasn't a mistake on your part.

Once you come into someone's world, once you perceive their language, you can better understand the person, and you can be more easily in communion and dance in the space of your relationship because you'll know where they're coming from, what it is they're saying, and how they feel. You actually enter into a whole new world.

The whole point is to meet them where they are. It's like the old saying about walking a mile in someone else's shoes. In this context, that saying would be translated as "Come share my world, come into my consciousness, and see what it's like to be me." When you walk in someone else's shoes, the intimacy created is so strong and wide that you feel their burdens and their joys. Intimacy is one of the most powerful means of human connection.

Years ago, I came across a book entitled *Black Like Me* by John Howard Griffin who decided to cross the color line in the 1950's. Using medication to darken his skin brown, he gives up his privileged life as a southern white for the world of the Negro. In one experience, Griffin offers a white woman a seat next to him on the bus; she replies, "They're getting sassier every day." It is then that he truly understands the weight of being a black man. For surely no white woman would sit next to a black man on a public bus. The lesson here is that sitting in other people's spaces can humble you and make you *one* with them in language and communication.

The greatest symbol of intimacy is the creator's relationship with mankind. This amazing entity was so in love with humanity that he himself decided to walk in the footsteps of man, in the confinements of physical flesh, so that he would have firsthand knowledge of what it was like to be those he was destined to redeem!

While on earth, he understood the language because, according to Christian scriptures— and if you're of the Christian faith, you believe this—he came down to be born of a virgin to walk with us as Emmanuel, God with us. In other words, he gave up divinity to establish intimacy with humanity. The writers of the New Testament named him the high priest who makes intercession for humanity. How could a divine being make intercession for a human being? By putting himself in their place and making an intentional decision to walk with them.

You see, if you want real intimacy, you must learn the language of your partner by stepping fully into his or her shoes. Know your language, but become fluent in theirs. Become bilingual. In today's education system, students identify their first language as well as any other languages they know. One of the education system's goals is for students to be fluent in other world languages, because this allows them to be more well-rounded and better communicators. It also expands their ability to connect with people outside of their first language.

Could you imagine visiting another country without being able to speak the language that's prevalent there? You would feel so out of touch and disconnected. Even if you knew some words in the language, you would still feel you didn't belong. Similarly, when we or others come to into a place (relationship) lacking the fluency of the language that works there, how could that possibly turn out to be worthwhile? It won't. Learn so that you may understand, and understand so that you may relate, and relate so that you may transform.

"In the space between CHAOS and SHAPE there was another CHANCE."

—Jeanette Winterson

CHAPTER FOUR:
BREATHE

The quintessence of life is encompassed in possibility. This is especially true when it comes to dating and relationships. It is possibility that causes us to feel that what we desire can actually exist. We date thinking that our dreams about love can and will come true. Most of us enter into dating under the impression that our reality will reflect what we have seen in the movies and read in books. We date pondering whether our daydreams will emerge into more than a sweet fantasy.

Considering these things, our expectation is that we will stumble upon the one who will be the flame that sets ablaze the warmest love we've ever known.

Perhaps she is the one that I met years ago as a butterfly.

Perhaps he is the one that I read about in a fairytale.

Perhaps this love will be a sweet dream that is unending.

Hope, though powerful, can also become somewhat daunting. Hope is the force that gives us desires we can't see but still dream of having at some point. If you hope long enough for something, it just might make you crazy; it just might turn you into someone you don't recognize.

Has hope ever been both a nightmare and a daydream to you? Has it ever been a bittersweet experience that you can't seem to live without no matter what it brings your way? That's what most of us have known hope to be as it pertains to our dating lives.

I sense that we, as humans, don't truly know how to deal with the daydreams and nightmares, so we stay asleep. The thought of waking up frightens us. The endless possibilities of being awake keep us in a deep coma that we voluntarily submit to. But why? I propose it is because waking up puts us on the court of life, leaving us with no other option but to play the game. It leaves us there to figure out what the next move should be in order to get the win we desire. Waking up forces us to deal with the sometimes hard truth that not every gift (person) is perfect, but it may be just what we need.

No, she might not look like what you thought you wanted, but she just may be exactly what you need. No, he might not make the right amount of money or drive a popular luxury car, but his heart may hold a love that you'll find nowhere else.

We all say that we have a particular type. In order for us to even consider dating someone, they have to satisfy every item on our criteria. Before we even consider taking them seriously, we have to first confirm that all of our standards are adhered to. So at this point, it becomes less about our hopes about relationships emulating our dreams and fantasies, and more about ideals.

But, have you noticed that many times you can get the type of person you want, and it still ends up not working out? Why didn't it work? Perhaps, when it comes to dating, you know too much about what you want and hope for and nothing, or not enough, about what you actually need. Yes, the possibilities are endless. Yes, there's a chance that your "ideal" person is out there, but what if what you are hoping for doesn't fit the design for your life? What if you're trying to force a reality that shouldn't be lived by you?

More often than not, deeply embedded in our hopes is the truth that we don't truly know who or what is good for us. Knowing what you want is not to be confused with knowing what is good for you. All too often, the two are very different.

Our hope should be driven by wisdom. When that happens, we start to search for people who truly complement us. A person who complements you well is someone who brings balance to the totality of who you already are. In other words, if I tend to be overly aggressive and insensitive, I need someone who can bring balance with their gentleness and sensitivity. You have to be able to honestly evaluate your character so you can wisely choose your mate. If you can't identify who you are (issues, traits, expectations, strengths, weaknesses,) how will you be able to determine what you need in a relationship?

Possibility is all around and presents itself in many forms. There is no set standard of what possibility should be. It's endless, it's boundless. The Bible teaches that you should be careful, for some have entertained angels unaware. An angel is a messenger. Perhaps you're rejecting the messenger because you refuse to accept the container of possibility it comes in.

We miss so many things that are right in front of us. The irony of this phenomenon is that the things we miss are the very things we hope for but lack an ability to identify when they arrive in a package that doesn't quite match our ideals.

Moment of Introspection: *How frequently do you entertain angels (possibility) unaware?*

The universe brings us things, but we often reject them because of our preconceived images of how they must appear before we can accept them. Gandhi came in a different image. Martin Luther King came in a different image. Both brought a message of possibility. The person that you met in Starbuck's, or someone you met at Bloomingdale's, or someone you bumped into on the subway could be the answer to unlock treasures you've never experienced before. Perhaps they are the one to cut the cord, so you might fly freely and soar high in realms you never imagined.

Possibility can be yours if you will let it be. It's in your very next breath if you take the chance to breathe.

Are you audacious enough to take the chance?

Or will you keep on entertaining possibility unaware?

"My life can be described in one sentence: *It didn't go as planned, and that's ok.*"

—Rachel Wolchin

CHAPTER FIVE:
TRAPPED IN TRANSITION

There is no such thing as a life without transition. Life is composed of beginnings, it has highs and lows, and it also has a future waiting to be explored at the appropriate time. The future could hold continuity or separation. In any case, the point is that life will have transitions as time progresses. The transitional periods of life will always leave us wondering, "Where do we go from here?"

Have you ever asked that question? Have you ever been asked that question? Have you ever been caught in the trap of transition, unsure of where your life will go from the spot you're currently in? Have you ever experienced an outbreak of life that completely catapults you into a sphere of confusion where you don't know what to do or how to move on? And what's so amazing—or perhaps difficult, depending on your personal perception—is the fact that you never asked or wanted to be in this space; it just happened.

Cancer *just happens.*
Termination *just happens.*

Car accidents *just happen*.
Divorce *just happens*.
Retirement and pension loss *just happens*.

As humans, we are never fully ready for any shifts that occur without our permission; in fact, I might add, with or without permission, life continues to do just as it pleases. There are so many illusions we create to give us a sense of control. Some people believe if they pray three times a day, they will accomplish a certain peace (control) of life, and others use financial security as a buffer against any unpleasant set of circumstances.

To be truly honest with you, it is impossible to have full control of the transitions that time will bring along the way. Unfortunately, that's not how the game of life is played. Many people are obsessed with control. Maybe you're one of them. Control freaks are common; these are the people who yearn for absolute control in order to feel like their existence is meaningful. Some are overly belligerent about having a sense of control. They typically show up to the table loud, with strong opinions and unreasonable terms and conditions. At all times, their need for control is evident and their manner overbearing. Do you know anyone like this? Are you that person?

World history teaches us about governments with dictators; some of the most famous were Adolf Hitler, Benito Mussolini, and Saddam Hussein. All of these individuals came in and took complete control. What is most interesting and uncanny are those of us who love to be in control, but at the same time have a strong passion, whether hidden or evident, to be controlled, Let's pause there and investigate *"a desire to be controlled" is it even possible?* I most assuredly think so and I'll tell you why.... When dealing with control, it normally presents itself to provide order from what could be something quite chaotic. Many times people will take control of a situation so that order might be established or restored. What I am about to say may seem quite crude or maybe homespun but, then again, this is why I wrote this. Being a lover of history, one of my most favorite periods has been that of The Holocaust. The backdrop of such a travesty and miscarriage of justice seemed to take place because of the lack of stable order due to Germany's defeat in World War I. Millions left pillaging for food, decent wages, and someone worth blaming, opened the doorway for the right perceiver of opportunity. That perceiver or master of control we come to call Adolf Hitler. What has fascinated me about this entire ordeal is not the man, but the masses. How does one man convince an entire nation to exterminate an entire race of people? How do moral, ethical, God fearing citizens drink an elixir that wipes away years of basic humane constructs on which the bedrock of society is built? The answer I have arrived at is the desire to be controlled. When a lack of control is present, there is a loss of security, and the fear of the unknown is made reality. You see, it's a lot easier to spread blame around than to accept ownership. When someone selling security in the package of control does a good job of it, we buy in and wait to accept the fruits of their agenda. Although many of us are rarely the front persons of control, we don't mind seeing others take the helm if we end up winning in the end. When asked after the war "were you aware of the camps?" many Germans were said to be "clueless and aloof" to the idea that such tragedies and travesties could exist. Or is that when the control works: *we accept and turn a blind eye to the injustices either known or unknown.* Perhaps the same can be said for America during the post war era concerning civil rights and African Americans. As long as the system of control worked to the benefit of the masses, it was widely accepted. Not until there was a breakdown of the system did certain consciousness become awakened to a new reality. It sounds twisted, yet it's the truth. We seek control. We take over countries for control. We take certain jobs for control because somewhere in our pursuit of control, we are convinced that it is intrinsically connected to power and it's truly what we want for ourselves. Perhaps we're in love with the power of control or the control of power.

In U.S. politics, we often find that every several years, the opposing political parties gain control of the House or Senate, which might mean a more liberal government or a more conservative one. All of this is of no consequence, because one only knows what actually gets accomplished. However, the illusion of that control causes networks to conduct countless campaigns, and millions of dollars are spent to influence people in the hope that these forums will win belief and support, which equate to control. Control seems to be the substratum on which many of our lives are built. There are some who are aggressive with their control, and others who are passive-aggressive. A passive-aggressive person subjectively attempts to control with a face of congeniality or an appeasing personality that disguises their true intentions. Nonetheless, being controlling is a vice that we all possess, whether knowingly or unknowingly.

It seems that life looks at our efforts to control and laughs. Life looks at our sense of order and finds such humor, such pleasure, because it understands that at a moment's notice, in a second, that control can be unraveled and disappear. In a moment, kingdoms and powers are shifted. A bullet can signify that, even with all of your security, you have no control. The knock at a door by two military officers with a folded flag can signify a loss of control. The doctor dressed in a white lab coat coming into the room with a chart and a message of doom can shift control, shift power. The bang of the judge's gavel with the pronouncement of a sentence can completely eradicate every iota of control.

And so we fight, and so we resist, and so a power struggle begins. That, my friend, seems to be the emphasis of this particular subject. How do we move from where we are to where we should be? Do we fight? Do we contend with what life is trying to give us? Where do you go when awakened by a midnight phone call informing you that someone you have loved since the beginning of your existence is no longer here? Where do you go when the person you've given your life to in a relationship says, "I can't do this anymore, I'm leaving." These are the moments of transition that crush the soul. When that happens, we are finally connected to the frailty of our humanity. It is in these moments that we connect with our finite being and the daunting reality that control is an illusion. It is here, my friend, that the vulnerability of our very existence is made clear. And though we have lofty mechanisms to shore up our sense of control, when life happens to us, they are blown apart. This is seen clearly in F. Scott Fitzgerald's novel, *The Great Gatsby*. Nick Carraway, the narrator, examines the lives of his friends. One in particular, by the name of Gatsby, has amassed a great fortune for the sole purpose of winning the affections of a high society damsel named Daisy Buchanan. He throws lush, plush, and Lucullan parties for the masses; which people come from all over the country to attend. All of this is done to get the attention of his muse, Daisy. We see the psychology and character of Daisy in a simple light when she speaks of her daughter, Pammy. "I hope she'll be a fool," she says. "That's the best thing a girl can be in this world, a beautiful little fool." Daisy wishes to imply that a woman has no worth in this world except to be beautiful and not terribly wise, and that mantra she lives out personally. Though she appears to be excited about that reappearance of Gatsby in her life, we find her own personal motivations are really at play. She wants attention, attention, and more attention. The consequence of that attention leaves an honest lover, with pure intentions "to have and to hold," dead in a swimming pool with a bullet in his back. The man who lives his life for another is nevertheless found dead alone. After great parties with hundreds singing his praises, no one shows up to mourn his early transition to the next world, not even his Daisy, who quickly ignores reality and lives out her mantra of being a "beautiful little fool."

Have you ever found yourself giving all for someone who couldn't return the favored emotion, even when you needed it the most? Or can you admit that you have been Daisy, a beautiful little fool to the real presence of life? The moment you answer those questions, everything changes…suddenly! You wake up a different person. You love a little differently. Your hellos have a greater cynicism and your goodbyes contain a hidden ambivalence to those you hold most dear.

Life is a gift, but living life is difficult. In times of constant transition, the answer to "where do we go from here?" is found in our ability to be vulnerable and willingness to adapt to sudden change when a mysterious finger leaves a message on our wall. That ability and willingness derive from a release of the need to be the ultimate governing force of our life and relationships.

What's at the core of this unreasonable yearning for control? The feeling that we have to protect ourselves.

With that in mind, the question then becomes, "What are we protecting ourselves from?" More to the point, what can we really protect ourselves from anyway? Can we protect ourselves from a broken heart? Can we really protect our loved ones from death? We can try, but do we really have the ability to do such a thing? You know the answer: no, you can't. And that has to be okay with you. You have to learn to submit to the truth that humans were never meant to have unmitigated control. While we can control some things, we will never be able to control all things.

Perhaps we should become vulnerable to the things we're attempting to be shielded from. Think about it for a moment. If you're open to hurt, you won't live bounded by the fear of it; and if you're no longer in fear of it, how will it harm you? What can hurt do to you when you have felt it, touched it, danced with it, and embraced it? It can do nothing at all. What can we extract from the experience of hurt but more strength?

I grew up in a classic fundamentalist sect, cult, denomination, or whatever descriptive word fits your particular world view. One of the main controls used was fear. We couldn't go certain places. We couldn't eat certain things. We couldn't integrate with the world we lived in because they were always afraid that the world would contaminate us to the point that we would no longer be distinguishable from the crowd. This was extremely important to them. The fear produced intentional avoidance. I was so afraid to be entangled in things that I became adamant about staying away from them.

But, what happens when life reels you in the direction of the very thing you're trying to avoid?

As The ancient faiths teach us about a man named Job who, during a recommendation from the Almighty, embarks upon a quest of the most horrid human suffering exclaims, "The thing that I had feared the most has come upon me." I believe that whatever you fear, you somehow connect with and inadvertently beckon to come to you. Some call it the Devil, some call it karma, or is it at all possible that it's just life. In whatever guise, fear has a subtle way of making what you resist gravitate toward you. We're taught all of our lives to be afraid of things. African Americans are taught to fear law enforcement. Caucasians are taught to be afraid of African Americans. Fundamentalists Christians are taught to be afraid of same-gender love. Where we go from here will be determined by the cancellation of fear. I've heard it said that ignorance is the disease and knowledge is the cure. You'll get to wherever you're going a lot quicker without fear, especially when you take the time to confront and be with what you are so afraid of. Where you will go will be determined by what you let go of; and fear has to be one of those things you release.

Someone once said that fear means "False Evidence Appearing Real," and perhaps that acronym rightly describes what I'm saying. You'll live life a lot longer and more successfully when you live the life you've been given without being ruled by your fear. The Creator has not given us a spirit of fear. Fear is a learned behavior that attaches itself to you. Many of us have been educated in fear. Well, it's time to cut that class, leave that school, and go on from there to a place where you are able to move freely. The possibilities are endless.

The freedom of possibility is available to you once you recognize all that can aid you in being more expressive. You'll not die from eating with someone from another race, you'll not endure the judgment of an evil deity because you engaged in conversation with a lesbian. Stop, stop, stop killing yourself so early. Don't you want to see what life is all about? Come out of the closet! Life is too short to die before your physical death. It is possible to experience a new lease on life once you become open to a new conversation in life. It all can begin with the language you use and the communications you engage in. So many of my greatest learning moments have happened when I took the time to be open to people who I would ordinarily never engage in any form of any communication. Yet, life comes and levels the playing field, so that where education or social status separate, life comes and makes you say "Hi, how are you today?" and the rest is history. Try it and see what happens.

"Some people are MAGIC, and others are just the *illusion* of it."

—Beau Taplin

CHAPTER SIX:
IT

My challenges and failures with sustaining and maintaining a relationship with the opposite sex constantly fascinate me. I've finally learned that I need someone who is secure enough in herself to be secure about me. Time has taught me the complexities of involving myself with someone who is insecure. Insecurities will always manifest in a relationship (of any kind). While it's easy to hide your insecurities by yourself, you won't be able to do so when you're trying to be in relationship with someone else. There's something about relationships that have the propensity to effortlessly call to the surface everything that people are concealing.

I've noticed that there are two types of individuals: individuals that have that "it" factor and those that simple don't. The individuals who have "it" are reflective of what Malcolm Gladwell writes about in *The Outliers*; they are people with distinctive personality traits that allow them to be great. Those who have the "it" factor do so because of circumstances beyond their control. To support his thesis, Gladwell looks closely at why the majority of Canadian ice hockey players are born in the first months of the year. He examines the "it-ness" of those successful in our world. Bill Gates, The Beatles, Christopher Langan, and others who have become one with their success, and he looks for the patterns for that success to see if it can be duplicated.

How do you identify someone who has "it?" Here are a few ways:

They know how to discern the rhythm of life.

They have a certain blessing or spirit that attracts people effortlessly.

They attract positive things; even when they walk into a room, they bring a certain energy that attracts people.

People with the "it" factor, as I have termed it, are one of a kind. There is something about them that is unparalleled. When you have "it," your way of being is compelling. I put emphasis on "way of being," because they have such an attractive presence that people find themselves talking to them and wanting to be in their space. People with "it" are extremely popular, which explains why other people want to connect with them.

When it comes to dating and relationships, almost everyone goes for the person who has "it." The average person wants to be with people who have the "it" factor more than they want to be with someone who doesn't. They want to be around them. They want to go out with them. They want to be in the entourage with them. They want to have them on their caller ID. They want to have them as a friend on Instagram. They want to share inside jokes with them. They want to be re-tweeted by them. They want to be acknowledged and affirmed by them.

Of course, none of these things are essentially a problem; but they become a problem when someone who does not have "it" cannot sustain a relationship with someone who does. In order to be in relationship with "it" people, one has to have a self-esteem level that can handle all the attention heaped upon the "it" people. You can't be instantly shaken and thrown off course by their fan club members or by everyone looking to be acknowledged by them. That often is the challenge with dating an "it" person.

Preparation is the key. It's wise to approach this sort of relationship with the understanding and expectation that it is going to require special work. The truth of the matter is that dating an extraordinary person demands extraordinary effort and dedication. Once you get "it," you have to know how to sustain it. If not, it'll crumble to pieces quicker than you can blink your eyes.

Moment of Introspection: *So, you say you're interested in dating the guy or girl who has "it," but are you prepared for all it comes with? Can you handle the pressure, or are you just enchanted by their persona?*

Pause! Now, let me say this, I'm not suggesting that someone who may not meet the standard of "it" within the context of this book is a person of no purpose and significance. Neither am I stating that anyone who doesn't have the "it" factor should be degraded or mistreated by someone who does.

Okay, back to the subject at hand...

I was on a date several weeks ago; we were out to dinner, and my date had asked me not to look at my phone. That's a reasonable request, so I obliged. I didn't have an issue with giving her that level of attention. I am learning that, in proper communication, you must commune with the individual. In other words, you must concentrate as you spend time with that person. Otherwise, you're just wasting time. You must turn off anything that could be a distraction, even if it's your own mind that tends to wander and think on trivial things that are irrelevant to the moment that you're in with that someone. When you mute the distractions, you create space to be fully present in that moment.

I took her request to mean that having a meaningful conversation was significant to her and something she could do masterfully. Thus, I gave her the green light to initiate our discourse. Now, that's a big move coming from me, as I am one to be very loquacious at times. Normally, I can initiate a conversation and do the engaging without any help. But I wanted this time to be different in consideration of her request; so I deferred to her. Immediately, I observed her inability to carry the weight of engagement and keep the attention of someone who has the "it" factor. Initially, she was able to stimulate me enough to get my attention, but she failed at consistent engagement. With individuals who have "it," there must be consistent engagement, or you will find that this person becomes bored and will eventually hire staff to do that job for them. Or, in other words, they will bring others to the relationship who will help maintain what it is you were to add but have failed to contribute.

UNDERSTAND THAT THERE ARE LEVELS

There are different levels of the "it" factor. In the same way there are different levels and ranks in the school system, so it is with dating and relationships. When we were in middle school and junior high, we started at the bottom, then we moved toward the top grade, and finally we were running the school, only to learn, after returning from summer break in September, that there had been a great metamorphosis and the level had changed…drastically. When you entered the walls of high school, you entered a new world. Though you had been at the top in the previous school, you now wound up back at the bottom. Why? Because the level of "it" you had some grades ago isn't the level of "it" for this new place. You're a freshman, and a freshman is just a freshman.

Life happens like that as well. The only difference is that in school, it is an expectation that you will change schools and be sent to new environments. In life, it's an option. You have the choice to explore possibilities outside your current community or circle. In other words, you control what you go after in dating and relationships. You also have to make sure that your level of "it" works for what you're aiming for. We can be "it" in our community or circle, but what about when we migrate elsewhere? Then we're exposed to the inevitability of starting over again at the bottom.

It is so often the common practice with both women and men that we strive to move outside of our community and circle, because we see something that's attractive with someone else. But when we arrive there, we are brought down to size when we attempt to decipher what it takes to live in that world, in that consciousness. It can be consuming and overwhelming when you realize the intensity of that community and come face to face with the fact that the grass is not necessarily greener on the other side.

When we arrive in places we aren't internally ready for, all our insecurities flare up. This leads to high expectations, as well as to many questions and uncertainties. You will find yourself looking for acceptance and affirmation. Everything is called into question, and all because you're on a level that you're not cut out for.

Do you really love me?
Do you really want to be with me?
Are you really interested in me?
Who is this person and why did they say this to you on Instagram?
Why does this person re-tweet you so much?

How can you tell if you're outside of your level/realm? You will know that you are when you're doing things that you once said you'd never do. Here are a few examples of those things:

- Going through their phones to investigate their emails and texts.
- Visiting their social sites to see who they're engaging, who liked their pictures, what comments are being shared.
- Invading their privacy to determine if they're as fully committed to you as they say they are.

All of these behaviors are certain indicators that you're in a zone you may not be ready for. When you behave in this manner, you prove that you may have skipped a grade you should have attended.

That can be challenging for both the person who has "it" and the person who does not. It is there that you see the dividing line that causes much frustration, because now there is tension that destroys the peace and oneness. Now behaviors are exposed that show a person's thoughts and fears being expressed through their actions and words. More often than not, it's words rather than actions. When someone is feeling "out of touch" or "out of place," it won't be long before their words convey their uneasiness.

What are you to do with those verbal manifestations of insecurity? Where do you go with them? At some point, it becomes a matter of affirmation, as you try to convince someone (maybe yourself) of something that you really have no control over. If you're the one with the need for affirmation, you have to be told that you are loved 320 times a day; you expect pictures of yourself to be plastered on their social media page daily; and you want them to brag about you to their friends and family. With all these demands and expectations, the unavoidable question is: are you actually seeking affirmation, or are you aiming for evidence to show outsiders that your place is real and secure so they'll look and deem you to have "it" as well? Do you want the affirmations for your own personal security, or are you marking your territory the way a dog marks a tree?

DO YOU?

What's your niche? When you focus on that, you're not really concerned with the superficial things, and you are more secure in your relationship with another person. The truth of the matter is that most of the individuals who find themselves over-exaggerating a need for attention and affirmation are usually out of touch with their niche. Your niche is normally your ability to be free from the contaminations of the "it" lifestyle and to simply be yourself, to have your own world, hobby, friends, focus, and so on. Having these things will ease the expectation for your significant other to do much to help you feel purposeful and accepted. This is how you provide your own security and safe place.

The consequence of just being yourself is that everything else will begin to flow freely without your having to force anything. I mean, to force something is to set yourself up for failure anyway. You'll never get an authentic role if you're trying to force it. Things that happen organically are the things that last; they are the things that actually mean something. By stepping fully into who you are and letting nature take its course, a favorable response from your mate is inevitable, and whatever you are seeking from them, they will begin to do naturally. They will invite you. They will bring you places. They will date you on your level. They will engage you intentionally. They will do all things in their power to satisfy you. Why? Because you've allowed nature to forge an authentic flow.

All you have to do is be the space for the flow to happen. You don't have to be anyone you're not or do anything outside of your character. We get confused because we try to promote, or to make, or to force things to happen when we don't have to do that. The reason why you were picked is because you were who you were at that moment, nothing more or less.

In order to survive in your partner's world, you must have your own world. You must give love and affection to yourself and find things that keep you happy and content. In doing so, you begin to find your reason for existence, which is not the same as anyone else's; you have your own unique and divine reason for being alive. You have to discover why you're here in the world. If you find your "why" and act on your "why," you'll effortlessly attract "it." People who are caught up in their own world often make the best mates because they have a separate world to share with another. It's a world that embodies their purpose, personality, and passions as an individual

Some people may not be on the grand stage of life, but that does not mean that their life has no purpose or meaning. Your life has great significance only when you find the purpose behind it. There is a river that runs inside of you, which I'll talk about in the next chapter. From this river flows all that you need to form a world.

Whatever your "it" is, own it, live in it, and others will be attracted to it.

Sophrosyne (n)

A healthy state of mind, characterized by self control, moderation, and a deep awareness of one's true self, and resulting in true happiness.

CHAPTER SEVEN:
MASTURBATE

A crucial conflict that is deeply engrained within culture and society is the inability to connect and relate to the world that encapsulates us. It has become increasingly common that people are not in sync with their surroundings. On any given day, while traveling to and from work, for example, you can observe a majority of individuals locked into their own world. They're there but they're engrossed in the music playing from their headphones, wrapped up in their latest Kindle read, or just caught up in their own thoughts while being totally uninterested in all that's happening in their vicinity.

    I must admit that, just a few days ago, I was filled with utter disgust at myself when I realized I was stuck on the subway without my headphones and would actually have to participate in the world. Now, if I were a true author, or at least one with the desire to spin reality in my favor, I'd tell you that some positive result took place from my misplacing my headphones that day, but that was not the case. As soon as I exited the train in SoHo, I made a beeline for the Apple Store to ensure I'd not encounter the possibility of having to actually talk to someone. Considering this, this passage resonates with me fully and completely. I'm guilty of being a social masturbator.

Why is it this way? It's because we have chosen isolation over engagement. We are so highly detached from the world we live in that it becomes hard to embrace even the idea of someone else. The concept of welcoming another is the furthest thought from most hearts and minds. Instead, many of us will spend this life loving ourselves and counting others out. While it appears to be satisfying, it is extremely unhealthy. We were never intended to go through life on our own, even though our system of isolation would have us believe otherwise. Humanity was created to dwell together in harmony, to establish bonds, and to make longstanding memories.

Rick Chillot wrote an article in *Psychology Today* entitled the "The Power of Touch." He states that "This is a touch-phobic society. We're not used to touching strangers, or even our friends, necessarily." He goes on to say that "If touch is a language, it seems we instinctively know how to use it. But apparently it's a skill we take for granted." It has been said that touch and communication are so important to the development of a child that their absence can cause death. Our sense of touch develops while still in the womb. What I find interesting is that as we age, our need for touch and communication doesn't diminish. Yet many of us attempt to deny the inner request for these things, and devise systems to reject the very things that make our lives full and satisfying.

It's so interesting to me that the system of isolation seems to be a well-oiled machine that just keeps going and going, It's a social front that is being further fostered by preachers, teachers, educators, and social media gurus, all suggesting that being secluded and shut off from the world is both healthy and acceptable. The fostering of this social front is perpetuating the mindset that created the system in the first place with adages like "In order for elevation, you must experience isolation;" or "A girl doesn't need anyone who doesn't need her;" or my personal favorite, "I was born without you, so obviously I don't need you to survive." Each of these mindsets and similar ones keep us on our personal islands.

It is sad that we believe we can live our lives successfully alone. I can't help but wonder if we truly understand the curse of isolation. Isolation isn't a form of self-love; it's a thief that robs us of the beauty of connections. The truth is that isolation only isolates one to be married to oneself. Eventually, isolation will mutate into bitter loneliness. Regardless of your efforts to think it is sweet, it will remain bitter.

How does one even arrive at the place where isolation wins? My guess is by forming fantasies. There has to be a fantasy in the mind that shows isolation to be a sweet and perfect reality; and that is why people become so engrossed in themselves. We manufacture these fantasies, stand on them, and live within the scope of them daily, all for the sake of self-pleasure and self-satisfaction. The act of forming fantasies that foster isolation is analogous to forming fantasies during masturbation. The expected end results with both are pleasure and satisfaction.

Let's look a little bit closer at this idea. I'm quite sure we all know what masturbating is and are well acquainted with its medicinal benefits. (That was a joke; smile!).

In order to masturbate, you must first have an image in your mind with which you can become intimate enough to produce an ejaculation (pleasure; satisfaction). Without this image, there will be no ejaculation; or if there is one, it won't be as pleasurable and satisfying as it would have been with an image to stimulate the moment. In this same way, social masturbation is accomplished with certain images. We become intimate with the idea of isolation and do whatever it takes to be pleased and satisfied with being isolated. It's all a mind thing! We have become masters of baiting ourselves.

What makes the mind able to internalize something and create a strong sense of stimulation? We have stimulated so much with our mind. We have stimulated fantasies that appear so close to reality that they produce pleasure; we take imaginary figments from an intangible world that manifest in tangible ways within our personal realities. If our minds can create such results with sexual and mental stimulation, how often do we as human beings create fantasies in the invisible world and make them believable in the tangible world? Very often indeed. Our minds are the master baiters, and they use isolation to entice and manipulate us, making us loners who completely dismiss the world around us and those who occupy it. Consequently, there is a weakness in our armor when we attempt to date and seek relationships, because we are too absorbed with ourselves to relate to and connect with anyone else. Dostoyevsky brings this concept to light very eloquently. In *The Brothers Karamazov*, he writes: "Above all, don't lie to yourself. The man who lies to himself and listens to his own lie comes to a point that he cannot distinguish the truth within him or around him, and so loses all respect for himself and for others. And having no respect he ceases to love." This seems to be the state or perhaps the result of the fantasy world we have created. How can you intimately and authentically love or give of yourself to another, when you cannot *distinguish the truth within*. How is that relationship to flourish? By what means will it grow? Grow it will, but what will it grow into? When the seeds of lies, mistrust, and ego are used to create, you create selfies and an entire consciousness that evolves and revolves around *you*.

You know what is most ironic? Ninety percent of the individuals who isolate themselves have a subtle yearning to be connected to the world around them. Their issue is that yearning will never be fulfilled as long as they shut themselves off from possibilities. You can't deal with the person in front of you if you're immersed in a cycle of self and loneliness. When you're so caught up in your consciousness, it doesn't leave room for anything new. The remedy for this epidemic is to be bold enough to step outside of your own world to create one with someone else.

EXIT THE STANDS—GET ON THE COURT

In order to be with someone, you're going to have to come out of your insular world, come out of the trap of your mental thoughts, and find your rhythm in the real world where things actually happen. There's a big world right on the other side of your isolation, but you'll always be a stranger to it as long as your mind continues to convince you to be secluded, separated, and guarded.

Maybe you're a master baiter, and your mind continues to be the bait that convinces you to give into pulling away from engaging society by accepting the shallow pleasures of isolation. Well, I want to challenge you to engage life differently. I dare you to open yourself to relationship between you and others. I dare you to travel into other people's space with a vulnerability that exposes you to their feelings, pains, and joys, to the essence of who they really are.

Sitting in the stands of life precludes relationship. For this reason, you should leave the stands and get on the court. That takes courage, but you'll later thank yourself for making the investment.

When you are in a relationship, you explore the nature of being and experience the evolution of oneness. Not only does the person you're in relationship with become better, vulnerable, and protected, but you also begin to feel new as a result of being with that individual.

When humans come together; there is true relationship, whether it is with your neighbor, your co-workers, your family members, or your significant other. You must come out of your brain, out of masturbating with yourself, and allow someone else to drive. Trust someone enough to take a stand for your life and you can take a stand for theirs. Let the universe find you in a place ready to receive, ready to move from the space that you're in now, to a higher consciousness that includes a larger world, one that does not maintain isolation, but promotes community and connection.

Every person you see and meet is a form of God in another image. And to love them is to see them as God intended. To behold humanity is to behold God's handiwork. Why wouldn't you want to willingly embrace that? Your answer to this question will determine whether you will live in a selfie world or a connected world. I'm hoping that the latter is your portion.

"I wonder how many people I've *looked* at all my life and never *seen*."
—John Steinbeck

CHAPTER EIGHT:
WHERE DO WE GO FROM HERE?

It seems as if you're not really living in our modern society if you're not connected to the world. If you're not present or aware of what's "in," it shows just how disinterested or disengaged you are from the times that we are living in. This is the age of social media; so to be connected, that ideally means that you're an active user of social media in some form. Social media is the face of this generation. Just about everyone has Facebook, Instagram, Twitter, Google Plus, Tinder, SnapChat, and a host of other accounts that suit their social needs.

I'm telling you, there's a platform for everything. Want to connect with other farmers? Want to mingle with Christians who are single? Want to find a hotel for your puppy while you're on vacation? Looking for an entrepreneurial gig to earn some extra income? There's a way to connect in each of those categories. It's amazing what the click of a button can do. It's even more amazing—and sometimes frightening—that such platforms make it easy for people online to be different from who they are in real life. Our culture has created an environment in which people can live out the fantasies of their mind, even when those fantasies are contrary to their true nature.

Beyond being able to portray a false identity, social media platforms have made it entirely too easy for people to take on the mindset that suggests that they have "arrived" or acquired a high level of importance that places them on top of the world. With several thousand followers, you can now become legitimate in your quest to be viewed as somebody popular or famous. God forbid if your selfies garner a lot of likes! Then you've really become somebody spectacular in the social media world. I am often fascinated by how prevalent selfies are as I browse through my news feeds. I'm not exempt; I take just as many selfies, and I do enjoy all it takes to get that perfect selfie that I know, without fail, will get the attention of my followers. I mean, we're all guilty of doing this, right?

I was in the mall several weeks ago and picked up a selfie stick for a friend of mine. This is a device that allows you to get a better camera angle for your selfies. Initially, it seemed like a brilliant idea. A deeper look, however, showed me how our world has become such a self-centered environment, where the celebrated selfie means so much to so many. Selfies are everywhere. Politicians and actors, preachers and teachers, even homeless people have mastered the art of the selfie.

Don't get me wrong, there is nothing wrong with selfies. I believe there's a lot of good in the fact that people don't mind sharing a piece of themselves with the public. However, it becomes a bad thing when more emphasis is placed on the superficial aspects of selfies—hoping for a lot of likes as a means of validation and letting the measure of your worth be tied up in how people view your selfies.

Moment of Introspection: *What kind of person has social media turned you into? Are you numb to society and the things that actually matter?*

Could it be that lack of connection is an inherited trait? After all, when we are born, our umbilical cord is cut, detaching us from our mother's womb and releasing us into life as our own individual. Human beings are born with a natural inclination to disconnect, or be disconnected from something. Perhaps this has, in some strange way, become deeply embedded within our makeup. Consequently, we stick to ourselves and limit our connections in the world to a few good selfies and a social media presence. While social media has its place, I'm afraid we have dismissed the idea of connecting in a more personal way with one another. Does this generation know anything about physical intimacy or mental stimulation? When was the last time someone turned you on without an Instagram "like" or flattering "shout out" post? Can you recollect the last time you had an extended, face-to-face conversation with someone that felt like minutes because you were so invested in the moment? Most never get to relish such simplicities because selfies and social media are all we've allowed ourselves to know.

Again, social media is good; but there's so much more on the other side....

SOCIAL MEDIA ISN'T THE FIX— NEITHER IS GOOD SEX

My observations have made me aware that many people use selfies and social media to quench the desire for real connection. It's similar to taking medicine that's supposed to be a cure but turns out not to be. Either social media is making people more self-centered or it's preventing them from being in touch with real people and having real engagements. In some cases, it's a disastrous combination of the two.

Social media isn't the only thing being used to quench the deep desire for connection with people; sex is, too.

SEX me real Good

Sex is believed to be an effective way to build a meaningful bond, but that idea is mistaken.

On many occasions and by many people, sex is used as a tool of intimacy and oneness shared between two people who have acquired chemistry with one another, although the chemistry may be strictly sexual. In the latter case, the sex is just two people having "a good time" and not "making love." A good time is simply enjoyable sex, while making love involves two people with a mental and spiritual bond coming together to express their love with the use of their bodies. You haven't made love with someone until your bond with them is realized outside the sheets and beyond the intense moans and pleasure. Making love is the closest thing we have to magic. Let me also state that the making of love isn't something confined to or defined by what happens between the sheets; that is only one form of the expression. It's the joyful anticipation that makes you rush home from work to see that special someone, or the craving for kissing that infuses first your head and travels to your lips as just the mention of their name sends warming chills through your body.

At one point, it was thought that men alone engaged in casual sex without emotional connection; now, however, women are doing it as well. They have even adapted the lingo attached to this behavior. You can find them saying things like," "I just wanted to get myself off, or "I just needed it tonight." While that may be part of their intent, there's another factor that's dwelling beneath the surface. In addition to wanting to just "get off," there's an inborn yearning inside of women and men that wants more than a good screw.

> They want to be held at night.
> They want to be understood.
> They want to share something real.

Scott Disick remarked about his girlfriend, Kourtney Kardashian, "I'll say after all this time and all these years we've been together, she can still surprise me and still lighten up my day and my heart." No matter what you think of him or their relationship, all of us have an indelible urge to be accepted and loved in this very way. Though life can often insulate us from the advances of others trying to love us, one must go deeper and be free to feel.

At the end of the day, no matter what people say and despite the personas that are used to paint a picture of contentment, nobody wants to be just a booty call or seen as the guy/girl who's only good for casual sex with no strings attached. Casual sex is good in the moment, but when it's over, the void remains. Good sex can make your toes curl, but it can't satisfy you emotionally, mentally, or spiritually. Only a true bond between two souls can satisfy the complete person. In all actuality, the traditions of most monotheistic religions taught against pre martial sex, and quite serious punishment was given to those who broke those commandments.

I often struggled with the concept, because I couldn't see the fairness in what seemed to be such an archaic and confining idea. It finally dawned on me that what appeared to be restricting and binding was actually the passport to "a whole new world." In ancient middle eastern times, the concept of marriage wasn't based on the parameters of what we call Love, but rather what made marriage the firm binding and grounding foundation was the word AGREEMENT. Two individuals would come together and agree to become "One." The unity of their agreement became a visible manifestation to the world that no longer were either of them separate entities or uncovered souls that could be explored by random spectators. But now they are free to explore each other with the assurance that what will be exposed and opened will never be used against them for harm. This then begs the question: who are you in agreement with? And if the person making the agreement has the capacity for such an agreement?

> Can I trust you upholding and protecting our agreement?
> Will you let others dictate to our agreement?
> Will your emotions distract you from our agreement?

Sex with no agreement is merely and sincerely unprotected sex…

And we are all aware of the "dis-ease" that comes from unprotected sex...

Let me also add that there is no real agreement unless both of you have equally agreed to this Union. One cannot be forced or coerced into it. One cannot be manipulated or tricked into it because when that happens it only creates a false sense of reality that later manifests itself in nightmares in day light.

I learned in Rob Bell's book, *The Sex God*, that the word sex finds its roots in the Latin word *secre*, which means "to separate." Again, we find reinforcement that sex is a tool that is frequently used to attempt a connection, but it rarely succeeds in doing so. Sex only accomplishes the shallow things while leaving the more important act of intimacy untouched. Selfies seek only to satisfy an area within us that longs for acceptance, and sex only looks to reconnect to what we no longer feel connected to.

So, what do we do?

What really matters?

Learning to let go can be one of the most freeing acts of your life. Many of us behave as if the world is against us when, in reality, it's you against yourself. You're the prison that has locked you away from the vast world that is your true self. The only thing you have that nobody else has is *you*—your voice, your mind, your story, your vision. This world deserves to experience that, but even if they refuse to feature it in

Time magazine or put it on the cover of *Vanity Fair*, you deserve to see yourself as undeniably free.

While strolling through Manhattan's financial district, I walked passed Ground Zero. I came across the 911 memorial building and was mesmerized at how enormous it was; it seemed to reach right into the sky without any effort. I saw the distant window washers going from window to window and cleaning each panel meticulously. And the thought came to me that this is how we begin our lives, with a fresh, clear panel reflecting only divinity, so clearly and effortlessly. Then, we begin to live.

> We meet our family.
> Have our first crush.
> Fail our first test.
> Get passed over for the varsity team.

And the list goes on and on, but each encounter leaves a fingerprint that eventually has to be wiped away so the surface is clear once more. Have you ever seen a car full of kids whose windows are smudged almost to obscurity? That's us! Our mirrors are filled with fingerprints of everything we've let touch us. Whether good or bad touches, they all leave impressions on the windows of our lives. So when you look into the mirror to see yourself, you can't because you're smudged with broken hearts, letdowns, divorce, bad business decisions, phony friends, and so on. All the fingerprints have left marks and when the sun shines, it magnifies the smudges.

What is the sun? The sun is love, a love that isn't trying to abuse you or make you feel unwanted because of your flaws, but the total opposite. Sometimes love doesn't come into your life peacefully. It arrives and puts you into a space called inquiry. It marks the before and the after in your life. It transforms you from a mere human to a spiritual being having a human encounter. Love shines through your window and exclaims, "I just want you and that's it—all your flaws, mistakes, smiles, giggles, jokes, sarcasm, everything that you are."

Let me introduce you to yourself today…

Allow these pages and these words to wipe away every smudge and every fingerprint. No, you may never forget the yesterdays but you can still be a reflection, a perfect reflection of the divinity that resides in you. The wealth of history in you can be a medicinal ointment to those feeling trapped in their own tragedy. You can be healing for someone's heart. But not until you tap into who you are…despite everything that you feel disqualifies you from being good…There's no need to hide or be ashamed of what stained your windows; you still have a chance at something new.

My friend, broken crayons still color, and there are plenty of books for you to color in.

The expressed selfie is one that doesn't need the approval of the masses; but I can tell you, it will draw them like moths to a flame, because they too are looking for a pathway to freedom. The expressed sex begins with an organic appreciation of yourself that, of course leads you to connect with your partner so intensely that you hear the silent conversations of their heart and feel their presence miles away.